The Unleavened Bread Cafe:

Twenty Years of Living Water

The Unleavened Bread Cafe: Twenty Years of Living Water

Editor, Wendy Vergoz

Intern Editors: Sara Frye, Abby Henderson, and Erin Rosebrough

Editor: Wendy Vergoz
Unleavened Bread Cafe Women's Writing Workshop
wvergoz@marian.edu

ISBN 978-0-9962998-3-1

Photography by Hannah Sobhie
Portrait of Elease Womack by Lily Carlsen

For Elease Womack, Einar Stefansson,
Tom Strotman, John Mills,
and David Metzger

And for Johnnie B.

Acknowledgements

Special thanks to Marian University, the Indianapolis Public Library, and Printing Partners for making the publication of this book and the accompanying reading possible.

Thanks also to Lori Arend, Hannah Sobhie, Peter Matsoukas, and Ellen Whitt.

Table of Contents

Foreword

When telling the story of the Unleavened Bread Cafe, Elease Womack quotes Ezekiel 37:3 which asks, "Can these bones live?" The metaphor Elease evokes through this question extends beyond its original application to the dilapidated building which would become the Cafe. When applied to the people who enter, the metaphor becomes a different question: Do these lives matter? Elease's answer to that question is an unequivocal Yes. Every action she takes, every word she speaks is an affirmation of the value of those she meets.

As visionary and proprietor of the Cafe for twenty years, Elease has met countless people seeking refuge, meaning, and hope. Elease, however, is so much more than a proprietor, and calling her that overlooks the fact that most who know her call her Mamma. *Mamma. Mother. Ma. Mother Elease*—the variations are many but the meaning stays true: Elease offers unconditional love. She doesn't judge. She meets people where they are. She offers love to them, no matter where or who they are. She believes in them.

In Elease's words, the Cafe reaches out "to the people who are broken and downtrodden," people often suffering as a result of systemic oppression and injustice. The Cafe gives those who are homeless food, and even provides them with a place to shower. And despite its meager budget, if people don't have any money, the Cafe feeds them anyway. Elease's passion for helping extends, especially, to women who are coming off the streets, women who have been prostitutes or have served time in prison—women in all forms of recovery. Elease knows that it is "hard for women coming out of prison with felonies to find jobs," so she welcomes these women, offering them her compassion and her belief in them.

I met Elease in October 2014 when a student of mine led me to the possibility of starting a writing workshop at the Cafe for the community's women. Our workshop, called Finding Our Voices, Writing Our Futures, started the following summer and culminated in October 2015 with the publication of *Voices Unlocked: Soulful Stories from 30th and Central*. As we worked on that first collection, the writing workshop transformed into a sisterhood. That sisterhood has only become stronger in our work on this second book, as has my admiration of the women's creativity, insight, and resilience.

There are moments in life marked by unmistakable grace, and I have had many of these moments in my work with Elease, my Cafe sister-writers, and my Marian University interns. Last fall we studied Lucille Clifton's poem, aptly named "sisters." During our discussion, across the length of two long tables, Kim remarked to Jackie, "We family. Not from the same blood, but when you speak, I listen." Kim's words stopped time for me, and grace entered that space. The beauty of this statement—the love at its center—stayed with me. Kim's words showed me that the act of listening defines what love is. True listening upholds and affirms the person speaking while simultaneously drawing that person nearer, transcending the bonds of familial blood. Thank you, Cafe sisters-writers, for all that you have given to me and to my interns.

Clifton's poem ends with the following two stanzas:

me and you be sisters.
we be the same.
me and you . . .

be loving ourselves
be loving ourselves

The Cafe teaches us to love ourselves, something people often struggle to do. How does it do this? Through Elease's sweeping, unconditional love. She welcomes all to her table, and it is no accident that the round table is her favorite: the table with no head, no place to exalt a leader. This table, though, has a true center, a center of living water running over with kindness, warmth, and acceptance, for Elease recognizes the innate worth of every individual she meets. Stranger or friend she welcomes them, an action deeply rooted in Hebrews 13:2, "Be not forgetful to entertain strangers: for thereby some have entertained angels unawares."

Over the last three years Elease has extended her love to me and my interns, as well as her belief in us. What enormous faith she has shown us, trusting us to write the story of the Unleavened Bread Cafe. This project, so much more than a book to us, reflects the respect, affection, and devotion we feel for the women writers. The spirit of the Cafe embraces us and the sisterhood of writers continues—young or old, black or white, from the academy or not, none of that matters—for we are woven together in purpose, by a desire to share a bit of ourselves and to celebrate the gifts that each individual brings: *we be loving ourselves / be loving ourselves.*

I want to especially thank each of my interns without whom this book would not be possible: Sara Frye, Abby Henderson, Erin Rosebrough, Hannah Sobhie, Lori Arend, and Lydia Godsil—all of us interwoven by so many moments of wonder and devotion, laughter and delight. I admire and love each of you.

What does this book celebrate? That Elease has given her life, given it unwaveringly, graciously, and literally—a full twenty years of it—for others. In 1987, Elease had a dream to open a cafe in a struggling community, to bind up the broken and bring hope to the hopeless. In 1997, the Unleavened Bread Cafe opened its doors. Here we are twenty years later.

Can these bones live? In a neighborhood marked by poverty, segregation, and systemic neglect, Elease Womack and her ministry teach us that there is life in these bones, these lives matter—the grieving, the lonely, the forgotten. *When you speak, I listen.* As you read through the writings in this book, writings about the Cafe and by the remarkable members of the Women's Writing Workshop, may your heart be stirred, and may your act of listening to these voices open up new spaces of love within you.

Wendy Vergoz

Introduction

The Unleavened Bread Cafe is a place of refuge, hope, and unconditional love, feelings that are inhaled in the Cafe like the strong scent of its fresh coffee.

Before beginning our work as writing interns, we were not sure what to expect. The women had a thirst for knowledge that quickly became contagious. Sitting around a bunch of tables, eating pastries, we were able to witness the power of sisterhood; we saw the difference an extended hand can make and the ability of faith to transform lives. We have evolved from interns to sisters.

The Cafe's sisterhood provides a safe environment to be creative and express oneself among truly invested writers. The assumed purpose of our internship was to encourage the women to express their thoughts and experiences through writing; the Women's Writing Workshop instead reignited our own passion for writing as we witnessed how important it is in the lives of our sisters at the Cafe. Writing proves, time and time again, to be a worthy practice no matter where one stands in life.

When we come into the workshop, we know that we will be in the presence of women who have generous hearts. We have witnessed self-less love. We have encountered courageous women who have persevered despite hardening circumstances and trauma. It is amazing to be in the presence of these women. They are passionate about what they believe in and are not afraid to stand up for it. They are wise, strong, resilient, and beautiful. Thank you, workshop sisters, for all you have given us.

Elease, we would like to thank you for the opportunity to be involved with your ministry. We would like you to know how strong we know you to be. You are a selfless woman whose confidence is rooted in her faith. Your joy is contagious; your smile, radiant; and your presence, calming. Elease, your unwavering faith, your passion for serving, and your wisdom inspire us.

Erin Rosebrough, Sara Frye, & Abby Henderson

Thus says the Lord God to these bones:
Behold, I will cause breath to enter you,
and you shall live.

~ Ezekial 37:5

SARA FRYE

Elease Womack: A Spirit Who Binds the Brokenhearted

"I never try to exalt myself—God does that."

The Unleavened Bread Cafe is a place of hope, restoration, and peace—those words have echoed time and time again as the lives that Elease has affected remember their experiences there. Stepping into the Cafe is like stepping onto Holy ground, like walking into a church. You walk into the Cafe and immediately feel like you're at home, no matter your circumstance. However, much like a church is nothing more than a building without God, the Cafe is nothing but a building without the commitment and the vision of Elease Womack.

Elease was born in 1943 in Indianapolis, the ninth out of ten children. As a child, she was ambitious and positive, much like her parents. Elease was raised in a Christian home and her parents, Samuel and Johnnie B. Williams, took Elease and her siblings to Sunday school and church every week. Every night, Elease and her family would sit together and have dinner. Her family-oriented parents were strict but loving.

"The most influential person in my life is my mother. She was a lady of character and respect."

Similar to Elease's ministry today, Elease's mother was an active member of her community,

1

helping those in need during the 1940s and 1950s. At an early age, Elease followed her in mother's footsteps. When she was in school, she helped raise money for a toy-land ball, which provided toys to donate to Riley Hospital. She also worked with other charities to help children in need. Elease spent her summer breaks from school at Bible studies and summer missionary programs. She knew early on that she had a calling to help the less fortunate, and she was proud that she could make a difference in her community.

When Elease was in fourth grade, her school closed, and in 1950, she was part of the first class to become integrated at Indianapolis Public School #46. She remembers it as a good experience and was surprised at the compassion she received from her teachers. The school put on a play for Thanksgiving, and Elease played a Native American girl. She was excited for the performance because Channel 6 news would be there, and she believed that she was going to appear on national television. Elease was a good student all throughout school, and she loved cooking and sewing, so home economics was her favorite subject. Elease's father wanted her to follow in her cousins' footsteps and go to college to be a nurse. However, Elease started working right after graduating from Arsenal Tech High School, and he accepted her decision and supported her.

"I'm thankful for a serving heart—making people feel like family. Like they belong."

Elease graduated from high school in 1963 and married Robert Womack Jr. She started working as a nurse assistant at Wishard Hospital and helped tutor children in kindergarten for five years. After that, she worked as a caregiver for the elderly for fourteen years. She believes that she was blessed to have been able to provide care for these patients, for it allowed her to work during the school year and stay home with her three children, Tia, Lyndon, and Sherri, during summer break.

Elease never had a job that was not serving others. She loves hospitality and making people feel at home, like they belong. Elease believes she was privileged to have the opportunity to work in hospitality and care-giving, but she always knew there was more to come: she always dreamed of owning a Christian cafe. In 1987, a friend gave Elease a prophecy, saying, "I can see you owning a business." This planted a seed in Elease and she started praying about it, growing more and more curious about how and where she could best serve the needs of the people who were downtrodden and broken.

"I saw a vision of people, walking around in the spirit
needing hope. I saw the end of the dream,
but I didn't know how I was going to get there.
I felt the Spirit of the Lord churning in my stomach."

Elease tried to start a business on 22nd and Meridian, where her aunt had a shoe store, but it was not the right time or place. The door of opportunity slammed shut. Elease went home and prayed— praying about what community to be in, not yet believing she was equipped to step out. During this time, Elease heard inspirational radio sermons that spoke to her, telling her that her vision would return. As always, she stayed in prayer.

*The Spirit of the Lord is upon me, because He hath
anointed me to preach the gospel to the poor*

*He hath sent me to heal the brokenhearted, to preach
deliverance to the captives, and recovering of sight to
the blind, to set at liberty them that are bruised.*
~ Luke 4:18

The prophecies came in parts, until Elease, as
she puts it, felt the Spirit of the Lord upon her.
Something came over her, and she knew it was time to
heal the broken hearted. Einar Stefansson, a member
of Tabernacle Presbyterian Church, called Elease and
said he had heard about her vision of working with the
community. Einar frequented the Mapleton-Fall Creek
Community and had witnessed its drug deals,
homelessness, and violence. He believed that Elease
was called to help the area. Every Friday morning,
Einar, Elease, and John Mills, another founder of the
Cafe, would meet and pray for the community and for
direction. One Friday morning, Elease had a cake in
the oven when Einar called. There was a building on
30th and Central Avenue that he wanted to show
Elease—but first they waited on the cake.

*"This is how these lives are—broken. Walking around
in despair and looking for hope."*

When the realtor first showed Einar, Elease,
and John the building, it was a disaster. The ceiling,
walls, and floors had holes and there had been a dead
body in the alley behind the building. God spoke to
Elease, saying, this is how these lives are—broken.
From the beginning, the Cafe has helped the broken.
The community partnered with Tabernacle
Presbyterian Church and began cleaning up the
property and organizing donations. John Mills owned

a construction business, and some of the workers had substance abuse problems, but John allowed them to stay on his property while they volunteered their skill and time to remodel the Cafe. On October 21, 1996 the building was dedicated to the Lord, and the Cafe opened its doors. On February 8, 1997, the Unleavened Bread Cafe began its vital role in the Mapleton-Fall Creek neighborhood.

"I didn't push. I try to meet them where they are at."

Since the beginning, Elease and the Unleavened Bread Cafe have provided jobs for those in recovery, giving them a chance to adapt to life before being out on their own. Elease is the mother-figure who nurtures these women, prays for and with them, and supports them. She makes a cake every year to celebrate another year of sobriety in the recovery of the men and women she has gotten to know. The Unleavened Bread Cafe has hosted various substance abuse meetings, survival skill classes, Bible studies, parties to pamper the women, Thanksgiving dinners, and numerous other means of supporting the struggling members of the community—uplifting them, softening them, and providing them with much-needed hope. Elease has offered both sanctuary and resources to individuals seeking support. She has served as a lifeline for those who have struggled to overcome disenfranchisement, battling a legacy of neglect.

"It's been a faith walk, He said it would be.
We have a shoestring budget. When it gets low,
all I have to do is go lay on my face and pray
and He remembers His promise."

Elease is a woman of faith, love, courage, and strength. For the last twenty years, her faithfulness has inspired the community as she has helped inspire those who are broken and downtrodden. Elease was courageous enough to start a Christian cafe in a struggling neighborhood, and her strength has encouraged and supported countless individuals. Elease is a strong woman, a role model, a mentor, and a friend who serves, not for recognition or praise, but because it is who she is—Elease Womack is a woman who binds the brokenhearted, setting their spirits free.

The cafe reminds me of how Christ renewed people's spirits. Unleavened Bread is a place of hope, no matter how low the streets pull you down.

Hear, listen, "You will walk out of there with hope."

~ Claudine Jones

ABBY HENDERSON

Hope for a Downtrodden Neighborhood

Ashes of Abandonment

Located near the northern boundary of the Mapleton-Fall Creek neighborhood, the Unleavened Bread Cafe is situated in a developing community struggling to overcome decades of neglect and poverty, and to lower rates of crime and violence. According to the Mapleton-Fall Creek Neighborhood Association, current projects include graffiti removal services, public-approved art, neighborhood-based blogs, and neighborhood-engagement programs. For twenty years, the Unleavened Bread Cafe has provided shelter and jobs to people who have escaped abusive relationships and to people recently released from addiction recovery programs and from being incarcerated, providing a unique service to the community. Beginning in 1996, the Cafe had little direction and little funding to carry out the vision of founders Einar Stefansson and Elease Womack. It still operates on what she calls a "shoestring budget," but through Elease's faith and commitment, somehow she keeps the doors open. The Cafe exists in a neighborhood which has inherited years and years of neglect in terms of social opportunity and resources. The neighborhood is still far from receiving the attention it deserves. Nevertheless, the Cafe survives and engages in a truly remarkable relationship with its community, making it unique and deeply valued.

A History of Segregation

The establishment of the Unleavened Bread Cafe and its place within the Mapleton-Fall Creek neighborhood was a long time in the making. According to the local blog, "Historic Indy," written and operated by Tiffany Benedict Browne, the neighborhood was originally known as "Sugar Grove" in the 1840s and only consisted of a small Methodist church community. Commercial development entered the scene and persisted throughout the 1860s as the community expanded and transitioned from "Sugar Grove" to "Mapleton-Fall Creek." By the late 1800s, the community consisted of residences, a post office, a general store, and a school. According to the Mapleton-Fall Creek Neighborhood Association, large homes were prominent by the early 1900s—some of which are still standing today—as Indianapolis residents migrated to this new and stylish community. Along with the extravagant dwellings were many luxury apartment complexes. The popularity of the neighborhood grew due to its convenient location between downtown Indianapolis and Broad Ripple. People could reside here but easily access city life by automobile or public transit.

By the 1920s, residents of the Mapleton-Fall Creek neighborhood had their eyes fixed on homes to the north. The original prestige of the Mapleton-Fall Creek neighborhood had been surpassed by northern communities which beckoned with better roadways and means of transportation. Despite the aesthetic appeal and character of the area, people were still choosing to migrate further north because of the new development happening there. By this time, Mapleton-Fall Creek was fully developed and functional; however, the wealthy residents were seeking something newer and better. After World War II ended, the neighborhood gained many residents of a lower socio-economic status who bought the large and beautiful homes that had become decades old. During this time period, the community proceeded to grow, once again, gaining many businesses including the Indianapolis Children's Museum. But by the 1950s, the neighborhood had, yet again, faced some challenging decades which made the modern homes of the northern suburbs seem rather enticing. According to The

Polis Center's narrative history, "Mapleton Fall Creek," another aspect contributing to the vacating of the neighborhood was that in 1950, Indianapolis Public Schools were mandated to integrate. The entire history of the neighborhood, up unto this point, had been one of segregation.

In order to avoid racial integration, some white residents left the Mapleton-Fall Creek Community and sought school corporations which would cater to the racial prejudices unfortunately prominent in the era. The now-very-old houses of the neighborhood became available as rentable properties, which drew economically and socially disadvantaged people, people neglected and oppressed by systemic racism and social inequality. During the 1960s, white residency dropped from 98% to just 54%, according to The Polis Center. As the demographic of the neighborhood shifted, so did the ability to maintain the old buildings and homes. Home ownership declined substantially, businesses evacuated, and crime rose. Despite some efforts made by the city, the community's residents, and local churches to address the deterioration of the neighborhood, the deterioration continued.

An Eminent Hope

Elease had always hoped to open a Christian cafe through which she could minister. In 1987, she had a vision in which she offered hope and fellowship to a struggling community. She could see the end of this dream but was not sure as to how she would get there. Not knowing where to begin, she prayed. She asked to be guided toward a place where she could begin her ministry. Enter Einar Stefansson, a member of Mapleton-Fall Creek's Tabernacle Presbyterian Church (Tab)—a church committed since 1965 to be "a force for Christ in the heart of the city" (Gable). Stefansson had a vision to make a difference in Tab's community, for he saw evidence of its poverty and neglect when driving on Central Avenue near Tab. In 1996, Stefansson mentioned his desire to make a difference in the neighborhood to Cathy Cunningham, a woman who worked at the Mapleton-Fall Creek Development Corporation. Knowing of Elease's dream Cunningham connected the two, and when Elease shared her dream of opening a Christian Cafe with Stefansson, he suggested that she start her ministry in Tab's Mapleton-Fall Creek Community. Elease agreed that this was the place. Stefansson, John Mills, and Tom Strotman—all members of Tab—joined with Elease and founded a not-for-profit that would be known as "Interwoven by Jesus," for in their eyes, He had brought them all together. Elease reflects on the group's unique makeup:

> Einar is originally from Iceland, John Mills is from New Zealand, and—I'm looking at how God did this—me, a black woman, and then He had Tom Strotman, he was the attorney. It was the four of us together, that was really a combination, but it was the work of the Lord that did that.

These four people would make all executive decisions about the Cafe.

After forming the not-for-profit and deciding upon a location, the four members of "Interwoven by Jesus" held a meeting with some of Tab's members to address the opening of the Cafe. Elease recalls herself thinking, *"Lord speak through me, a black woman, in this room full of white people."* She told the group, "I know you all have your bachelors, masters, and PhD's, but I have my BA—born again!" The group from Tab supported Elease and Stefansson's vision, and this is how the partnership between Tab and the Unleavened Bread Cafe began, a partnership which continues today.

Stefansson came across a building for sale on 30th and Central Avenue, a building once owned by Southern Star Baptist Church. They had been there for twenty years but left for a location closer to downtown Indianapolis. The building, however, was in shambles, with holes in the floors and ceiling. Regardless, this would be the place where Elease and Stefansson's vision would be fulfilled. The members of "Interwoven by Jesus" and Tab, as well as people from the Mapleton-Fall Creek Community, began working on the reconstruction of the building. The Cafe was going to be given back to the Lord through the tireless efforts put into refurbishing it by Elease and those who contributed to making this vision a reality, many of whom, according to Stefansson, were homeless members of the community who worked for no pay, because "they just wanted to be a part of it."

The Unleavened Bread Cafe opened its doors on February 8th, 1997, with its first employees being women in recovery from drug addiction. Aside from serving breakfast and lunch, ministries offered included survival skills classes for women and Bible study groups. The Cafe also held free Thanksgiving dinners to get to know people from the community and let them learn more about its unique ministry. At Christmas, the Cafe would host parties for its community of women and their families, always catered by surrounding churches which also donated toys for the children of the families. Elease felt it necessary to offer the women involved with the Cafe some pampering. She said, "We needed something to soften them, the streets beat them up." Elease stands by the policy of always meeting newcomers to the Cafe where they are at. She never pushes any guest to accept her ministry, but she has always reminded them of the Cafe's presence and willingness to serve.

The Cafe has served the Mapleton-Fall Creek Community for twenty years. It continues to use hope to combat the neighborhood's heavy history. Elease channels her faith to uplift the downtrodden neighborhood. As the heart of the Unleavened Bread Cafe grows through experience after experience, so too do the hearts of those affected by its irreplaceable ministry. Though the community still reflects its history of neglect in terms of social opportunity and resources, the Unleavened Bread Cafe has proven for twenty years that there still exists an eminent hope.

Erin Rosebrough and Hannah Sobhie contributed to this story.

Bibliography

Benedict Browne, Tiffany. "Deep Rooted History in Mapleton-Fall Creek." Historic Indianapolis / All Things Indianapolis History. N.p., 19 Dec. 2016. Web. 23 Mar. 2017.

Gable, Rev. L. John. "History of Tab: The Tab Creation Story." Tabernacle Presbyterian Church. N.p., 2009. Web. 26 Mar. 2017.

Mapleton-Fall Creek Neighborhood Association. N.p., 02 June 2015. Web. Accessed 23 Mar. 2017.

"Mapleton-Fall Creek." The Polis Center, IUPUI. N.p., n.d. Web. Accessed 23 Mar. 2017.

Stefansson, Einar. Personal interview. 11 Feb. 2017.

Womack, Elease. Personal interview. 12 Mar. 2017.

Einar and Lena
Stefansson

The Cafe
under
construction

New Writings by the Women

me and you be sisters.
we be the same.
me and you . . .

be loving ourselves
be loving ourselves

~ Lucille Clifton

VICKIE ARMOUR

Fear to Strength

My girl power came from watching the strong matriarchs of our family starting with grandma raising momma by herself. Grandma, not ever knowing her father, learned to do it on her own with the baby she had at 16. Momma married Daddy at 17 and I was born when she turned 18. I can remember her saying, "You can do or be whoever you want to be, Vickie." That started the fighter in me.

You see, I was real scrawny in size so people bullied me and I never fit in. Growing up I had no siblings to protect me, so I had to learn to fight at an early age. As I grew older—grade school, middle school, high school, finally an adult, one abusive relationship after the next—my fear became my strength. Every man I got with wanted to control me and when I wouldn't comply, they'd black an eye.

I still kept hearing my mother say, "Vickie, you can do or be whoever you want to be." I still didn't know where my girl power was growing from. God illuminated what was instilled in me by my momma years and years ago. The words she kept repeating were, "You can do all things through Christ who strengthens you." The strength to say NO, the strength to let GO, the strength to say goodbye, the strength to know He is my source. Without His love for me, my strength would have remained a mystery: deep, hidden, and unheard. Today my girl power is His spirit living in and through me. I am finally me!

VICKIE ARMOUR

Vickie Armour went from being hopeless to hopeful by serving daily at the Unleavened Bread Cafe. She says, "Being in the writing class has truly blessed me. The women from Marian University and Professor Wendy helped me to express and heal at the same time as learning to write different styles."

CAROL EVANS

A Journey of Discovery

My world is once again beautiful because I have learned not to wear the mask. I know who I am and where I come from. I'm not an edited and decorated version of myself. I come from my fears, courage, mistakes and successes in life.

Yes, life has given me the best…loyal friends, rich experiences, and the ability to pursue my dreams.

Now, when life seemed unbearable and lost, I knew I had to truly learn to—once again—love myself, not fear life, and stop choking on my own uncertainty and pity.

It was going to be okay to have memories, good or bad, because they can be useful in teaching you about loss and your future journey. You can have a productive outcome. Yes. A journey I can and did literally take: to help sort out things about my life and to prepare me for that empty nest I feared with no partner.

I decided to get up one morning, catch the commuter train to Sacramento, and take a trip of discovery. Who had I become? Did I truly love me? I felt I would have the answers to my questions—and the strength I would need—by the time I returned, answers about whom and what I choose to become.

It was a gorgeous, sunny, and warm morning. The train would leave at 9:15 a.m. and return to Oakland at 5:30 p.m. When I boarded the train, it was practically empty; I took a seat in the lounge with a large table to spread out my newspaper and magazines I had brought to read. Through my large window, I had a picture-perfect view of the San Francisco skyline, the Golden Gate Bridge, and the imposing view of the Bay as the train rumbled down the track with that legendary whistle blowing.

When I arrived at my destination, I first thought about where I would have lunch. Many tourists were in Old Town, a popular spot in Sacramento, taking in the sights and visiting all the shops. The place I picked for lunch was a charming little restaurant by the water. The geese were flying and searching for food, people in their boats and on platoons, laughter and fun everywhere, reminding me about how beautiful life is. I sat on the deck having my lunch, under an azure sky.

I took a museum tour and went in and out of shops, met a few wonderful folks and their families, and once again enjoyed life from deep inside of me. "The spirit of the roses lived on in my heart." Just as they did in my short story, "The Roses: A Garden of Secrets."

Suddenly, I felt strong, determined, necessary, and needed by the world. Most of all I felt loved from within. Riding back to the Bay Area, I knew I could live my life without trepidation or doubt. I would honor my expectations no matter what others thought I should be or do.

Take off the mask and toss your fears, Carol, because you are going to be okay.

CAROL EVANS

        Born in Indianapolis, Indiana, 79 springs ago on April 27, 1938, she is the oldest of five children. She moved to Oakland, California in 1971 where she received her Bachelor of Arts in Sociology from Mills College. She now resides in Indianapolis. She is a published author, fund-raiser, community activist, and the founder of the award-winning calendar, "Positive Images of Oakland."

My Grandmother's Soap

We lived down the hill, by the canal where the railroad tracks passed through Freemansburg on the way to Easton and beyond. We could hear the rattle of the train cars as they passed on by, the engineer tooting the horn as it entered town. It was at the foothills of the Bethlehem Steel stacks billowing smoke that I made soap with my Grandmother for the last time in the fall of 1965, the year I was in fifth grade. This was the year that we moved.

Soap making was hard work, an all-day affair requiring skill, patience, and care—a process that kept us running from the big butcher block in the store to the summer kitchen and out into the backyard. My grandmother, the local butcher, trimmed the fat from the pig, and cut it into big, white, slippery chunks. We filled the buckets with the fat, carrying them to the summer kitchen to put in the big cast iron pot on the stove, a stove that I loved. It was a majestic 1930s gas chamber stove with stacked storage doors in a white porcelain enamel finish providing fried potato noodles, pork chops, and Sunday's roast chicken.

It was a big stove for a big pot to render pounds of lard to mix with lye and water for making cakes of laundry soap. Two batches of melting and stirring, adding and ladling from stove to galvanized tub in the back yard for molding and cooling the mixture, a thick white pudding. I stirred with the weak arms of a child, a pushing in of the paddle as much as a turning of the thick liquid. My grandmother, all 4'11" of her, barrel-bellied, arms strong for stirring and lifting and legs made for standing 12 hour days, waiting on customers and doing chores. After the soap was dry, she cut it into large cakes and we wrapped it in worn and tattered flour sack cloth.

My grandmother wore housedresses with cotton aprons from neck to calf as did most of the mothers in our section of town. Row houses, my grandmother's store smack in the middle, the store with boxes of Luxe and Tide laundry detergent on the shelves—the kind that we didn't use in our white enamel wringer washer with a blue trim.

UP THE HILL

We moved up the hill when I was ten. We moved away from the row homes with long narrow back yards and postage size front yards. We moved to the houses with big front porches for chairs or porch gliders, you don't see these things anymore. Families sat on their front porch watching neighbors walk on by. Up the hill the porches were smaller, the front yards bigger, and the people stayed inside more. We had moved into a neighborhood where ranch homes were preferred with sprawling yards, houses wider than deep in which everything happened on the same floor: the sleeping, the eating, and living. Mothers wore Bermuda shorts with matching striped shell tops. Women had their hair done on Saturday mornings, carefully wrapping their hairdos with toilet paper at night so that they would keep.

My grandmother wore a bonnet and our house had two floors and a basement. During the summer my grandmother would sit on our larger-than-average front porch and watch the children play in the street. My dad bought us an automatic washer, harvest gold, kept in the basement right next to the utility sink we hooked the wringer washer to on Monday mornings. Unwrapping a cake of soap, I would fold the frayed rags for some other use. After the tub of the washer was filled with hot water, I would drop chunks of soap into the water. We would wait until the machine finished agitating the mixture of lard, lye, and water before putting our clothes in: housedresses, aprons, work shirts, bell bottom jeans, and halter tops.

We bought our first box of Tide in 1972—two years before I went to college—the year the white enamel wringer washer was pushed to the far side of the basement by my grandmother, barrel shaped, with arthritic knees, and arms ready for the automatic washer.

ESTHER HORVATH-FER

Esther has been a friend of the Cafe for over 10 years. She joins Elease in ministering to the women in the community, enjoys cooking for and serving the seniors the first Tuesday of the month, and has loved road trips to the farm with David, Elease, Charlie, Jab and Joe.

Esther grew up in eastern Pennsylvania and has lived in Indianapolis for 32 years with her husband Ahmet. She is the mother of two grown sons: Danyal and Adam. She enjoys writing, sending cards, studying scripture, cooking, bird watching, long walks, and traveling.

DARJSHAI JORDAN

Amazing Grace

When I was 16, still new, I went for a ride with Ice Cream and Red. She said we could trust him, he's real cool. Should have went to the radio station even though we were running late. They said come on let's hang out it'll be great. So we rode around drinking Wild Irish Rose and smoking weed, stopped at the roller rink, then we continued to ride, smoke, and drink. Don't know where my mind went, it's too late. The time was spent. It was midnight, I can't go home, I thought. He said you can come over to my house you'll be safe, I have my own place. My girlfriend said come on, I'll go with you.

So we walked into his basement apartment. There were bars on the high windows, he locked the door and put the key in his pocket (the only way out). He opened a drawer and pulled out a gun. He pointed to a mattress on the floor (the only furniture in the room) and said what he wanted done. I became hysterical and loudly began to cry, and I was praying inside. My friend said let's just do what he told us to do so he'll let us go—so we did. Many years later I found out that young man was part of a ring of men that used to kidnap girls and take them to Chicago and New York and turn them into prostitutes, but for some reason, he let us go. He had also gotten saved and become a pastor. That's amazing grace.

Power and Strength

Where do I get my girl power?
Where do I get my strength?

I would have to say from
God and my Momma and
Of course, my children and my children's children
And my Ancestors too, and the memory of
All the things we have
Already made it through.
But the poets came to mind
Like momma Maya Angelou says
"Still I rise"
And sister Meri Evans
Says "I can"
Uncle Jesse Jackson
Reminding me that "I am somebody
I am special"
Brother Langston always says so much
About "My People"
And my cousin Marley's
Always singing in my head
"Don't worry bout' a thing
Every little things' gonna be alright."
Yes, so the words of the
Poets give me
Power and Strength.

DARJSHAI JORDAN

Supernova

Your Reaction to Who I am
and What I may have done

What you think I will be
or Who you Believe I will Become

are of absolutely No Relevance
Because the truth of me you
will Never know

you Don't know My Hopes, or my Dreams
my Pains, my Sorrows, or my inner Being

I am Light, I am Love, I am Creativity
I am Nurturing, I am Caring, I am Radioactive
I am Fruitful, I am Rain, What I Really Am
Cannot be Explained

I am like the Sun
I am a Supernova.

DARJSHAI JORDAN

I, Darjshai, am the mother of four daughters, and the grandmother to eight children. I like to cook, bake, sew, garden, and I also love music and the arts. I discovered writing and poetry at about the age of 10 or 11, and my love has only grown since. This writer's class has sparked something in me that has been waiting so long to come out. So here's a little taste of the inner me. I hope you enjoy!

A MIRACLE NAMED JACKIE

Firecrackers

One July 4th on the wall outside my apartment hangin' out with my son and Charlie, our neighborhood alcoholic, who was coming up the street and saw us sitting on the wall.

So he sat down and joined us on our wall.

Just about that time, all of a sudden and out of nowhere, fireworks went out all around us and continued on and on for quite some time.

The three of us sat there 'ooh'-ing and 'ahh'-ing at the beauty of the fireworks bursting in the sky above us.

That beauty, coupled together with the whistles, the blasts, the bursts, the pops of many different kinds of fireworks, mixed with the sounds of busy city street traffic passing by as we sat on our wall.

I can smell the sulfur from the fireworks as well as the gas and diesel and smut from the cars passing by, as well as the lingering smell from the grills from all the neighborhood barbecues.

An unexpectedly beautiful time in an unexpected place.

A MIRACLE NAMED JACKIE

Summer Break

School's out for the summer!

Everybody but me is packing to go home for summer vacation...

I sit in my dormitory room listening to varying degrees of excited laughter and joy and different conversations as my fellow students pack their bags while discussing their plans, reservations, swimming parties, slumber parties, camping—all of the traditional summer activities.

I'm not packing because "home" for me is the orphanage where I lived just a few weeks ago and the very last thing that I want to do after finally graduating high school and finally graduating the orphanage is to spend my summer at the very orphanage I've waited four years to get away from.

Thanks to all of my excruciating circumstances, all the authorities met and agreed to let me live in my dormitory room while summer break ends so as to not cause me to spend my graduation summer at the orphanage.

But as quiet as it's kept, all unexpected benefit arose while overcoming the huge wall of homelessness as well as surviving the loneliness of an empty dorm for a whole summer. The victory is that as the students started arriving back to the dorm—two arriving today, three arriving yesterday, two more the next day etc.—I was able to establish a bond with almost everyone, so much so that I ended up being voted, unanimously, to be the dorm's president for the freshman and sophomore years!

Addictions

Strange. How much they're alike,
    one to another.
Addictions, all, wear the same cover.

Be it shopping or food, work or TV;
Addictions, all, have the same purpose to deny
    one being truly free.

So addicted am I to my computer,
    my tablet and to my phone.
It's as if I've become a human drone.
When they sometimes temporarily go on
    the blink,
All of a sudden I can't even think;
I can't function, clueless with no unction.

Reminds me of crack— Boy!
    Was that a trip
If I couldn't get one more— man—
    How horribly I would flip-out—
    Incapacitated for sure
As helpless and as hopeless as the bait at the end of a
    fishing lure.

It was as if it was all that mattered,
my brain, without it, was totally scattered.

The power of addictions in our society

is something to behold—And
not frivolously—

For if you look closely, you will SEE
the mind-altering status that can bring
    you to your knees.

Strange to me how much alike they
are— one to another
Just as if they were brothers.

A MIRACLE NAMED JACKIE

"A Miracle Named Jackie" hails from Austin, Texas, but has been an Indy resident for the past ten years.

Today, thanks to the word of God, The Bethlehem House, and The Unleavened Bread Cafe, she is enjoying ten years clean and sober from crack cocaine addiction, and running a crack house and a prostitution ring, and all the madness that came with that.

Thank you so much Wendy, Abigail, Erin, Sara, Lori, and Hannah for your willingness and open-mindedness to meet me right where I am.

TAWANA PROCTOR-ROBINSON

Not Tomorrow But Today

I just want to thank you God for all that you do
I don't even have to prove anything to you
You love me just because I am your child
You loved me even when I ran wild
And for all that, I just want to say
That I surrender my life to you not tomorrow, but today
I want your will done in my life
I am tired and will not put up a fight
I seek to do what is good and exceptional in thy sight
God please help me to live holy and right
I know that I can't, but You can
If I just trust and put my hand in Your hand
Through temptation I can stand
Not just stand but come out victorious
In the end when we win it will be glorious
My life is Yours and I will give it to no other
Not even my father, husband, child, or mother
I throw my hands in the air and say
Lord my life I give to You not tomorrow but today
You kept me in times when I should have lost my life
You comforted me when I could not sleep at night
I know that You are real no matter what others think
In my own sin and destruction I could have sink
But, You held me like a new born child
Whispering in my ear this will be over in a while
The times when I rebelled and deserved to go to hell

Even when I was locked up and thrown into jail
I know it was You that brought me through
Those were the times when I did not know what to do
You knew just what it would take to put on the brakes
So that I would not have to pay for my own mistakes
You hid me so when hurt, harm, and danger came my way
I could live to try and get it right another day
God, You are my sword, my provider and my shield
Finally, my Father, I want to do only Your will
I'll take the first step and walk by faith and not by sight
Lord today I surrender my whole life without a fight
Yes, to Your will and to Your way
Believe me when I say my life is Yours not tomorrow, but today

TAWANA PROCTOR-ROBINSON

Tawana Proctor-Robinson is a loving Christian woman who always helps others. She enjoys watching movies, spending time with her husband, children, and church family, and writing inspirational poems.

GAIL REAVES

Grandma and Her Grandkids

I never grew up with a grandmother, and hearing other kids my age talking about their times hanging out with their grandmothers —cooking, going shopping, going to church with them—sounded like a fun time.

I was in my late twenties when my biological dad told me about my grandmother. I was excited to get to know her. She lived in Tennessee. I asked for her phone number. This began my journey with my grandmother. I called her up and introduced myself. She was glad to hear from me as I could tell by the excitement in her voice. I told her I was married with three children. I wanted her to see me and my family. I got her address and I wrote to her as soon as possible! I mailed her pictures. She responded back days later. She had a feeble penmanship because she was in her late 80's. But, what a joy! I can say, "I have a grandma! We corresponded a few times. I never made it down to see her. But, I looked a little like her, Grandma Trannie." She passed away a few years later. No, I did not go to her funeral. I just have great memories of talking with her and sharing my life with her.

I started having a desire that, whenever I became a grandmother, I wanted to be the best ever! In 1996 I became a grandma; I was in the delivery room coaching my firstborn daughter to hold onto my hand and to breathe slowly. I was pretty calm for her sake. And then as the doctors were there to assist the birth of my granddaughter, we cried, and rejoiced that little Synaria is here. When I held her, I just was overwhelmed with joy, I'm a grandma!

Synaria is now 20 years of age. I have had 10 more grandchildren. But one of my granddaughters was stillborn. I did not see this coming, to experience the death of a grandchild. I had taken my firstborn daughter to a normal routine visit. She was given a sonogram. We were in the room when the doctor came to tell us the baby was dead. We just cried in unbelief. And hugged each other.

They gave instructions that in a few days she would have to birth this baby who is dead. The sadness that we felt. A few days later in the labor and delivery room, the baby came out, and they laid her lifeless body in a container. I went to the baby, Janiyah was her name, speaking life that Jesus could raise her up, but He didn't. Later, we found out she wasn't fully developed in her body. A few days later, we had a service at New Crown Cemetery. Her great-granddad, Rev. Joseph Reaves Sr., and grand-dad, Joseph Jr., said words of encouragement to the mother and grandmother. I did not see this coming, to experience the death of a grandchild.

So, as years went on, I engaged my life to be the best grandma, buying candy, spending time, playing around with the grandchildren, taking them to parks, out to eat to McDonald's, hugging and letting them know they are loved. Then one day, my oldest granddaughter said, "You're the best Grandma ever!"

GAIL REAVES

Mrs. Gail Reaves, was born in Indianapolis, Indiana on May 27, 1959 to Estella Woods and Jessie Rainey Sr. She has seven sisters and five brothers, but one is now deceased. Gail has been married 35 years to Joseph Reaves, Jr. They have two daughters and one son between 33 and 39 years old. Gail is a proud grandma to eleven grandchildren, one who was stillborn. Her grandchildren range in age from four to twenty years old.

Gail has assisted her husband in ministry as the assistant pastor of Greater Faith House of Prayer for sixteen years. Gail loves working in the Mapleton-Fall Creek area with her husband, reaching families, and especially evangelizing to the children about Jesus. Gail works as an infant teacher at Little Duckling. She loves nurturing, caring, and playing with the babies and teaching them nursery rhymes.

LYNDA SKIPPER

Irreplaceable You . . . in Life

Everyone counts. You will have struggles and unbelievable sheer jubilee moments in life. That phrase, "Life is not a rose garden" is reality. If someone told you that life is like a dress rehearsal and you can come back to life and get a do-over, they lied to you.

Getting back to the struggles, you will surely them have in life. Let's deconstruct the previous sentence by focusing on two words—in life. The struggles will always be with you, me, and all you meet on your journey. It is only in life you can experience all your moments of sheer jubilee. In your death, it's too late to recognize that you were irreplaceable.

Imagine a bus exchange center. There are many buses with different destinations. Well, it's up to you to choose the right bus. If by chance you find yourself on the wrong bus, then you need to find the strength to get off that bus. At the bus exchange center you will find buses driven by couples, called Mr. and Mrs. Alcohol, and it is no surprise they guarantee a good time. Irreplaceable you, we find sitting in the back of the bus drinking confidently that all is well. Ask yourself, who are you kidding?

In my case, my father started drinking as a teenager and continued throughout his adult life. He did go to rehab several times and did stop at the end. You are second to no one in life. I lost my father to alcoholism when he was 45 years of age, while I was growing up in Mapleton-Fall Creek neighborhood just three blocks from the Unleavened Bread Cafe. Both of my parents worked hard to give us a quality life, setting limits with high expectations. I'm sure my dad, who was a truck driver for the city for 18 years, never intended to lose his life leaving behind his wife and children.

Many people find discussing mental illness to be a taboo topic of shame. Well, I am not ashamed to discuss it and I have observed mental illness upfront for decades. What I know is there are treatment plans for mental illness that are working, along with many new resources. Seek any help you need with your head held high. You do not owe anybody an explanation or apology: your job is board the right bus. For those who seek to shame people for developing mental illness, surely you must know they had nothing to do with developing their mental illness. This is a condition they must deal with all their lives. If you still find yourself mocking them as crazy or crawling under a rock if someone mentions mental illness in a family, I suggest you find something constructive to do with your life. Don't waste your time underestimating what people with mental illness can do or their capabilities and achievements, because you are in for a rude awakening. I am a mental health advocate. Again, know there are more than enough of us who believe in their recovery and their ability to live a productive life. We have seen it happen time and time again.

Without treatment for your mental illness, over time you may find yourself losing your will to live. This is what happened to one of my family members. Yes, after two years of trying to manage all those incoherent thoughts alone, it had taken all the strength needed to fight and manage life. When you lose hope, you can ask for help to tie a knot in the rope and hold on because you are Irreplaceable. Nobody can take your place. God created you as a unique gifted individual. Our job is to get busy living.

There is a special place at the corner of 30th and Central Avenue—The Unleavened Bread Cafe. Many buses are waiting for you at the Cafe in the form of programs and people with a deep connection to loving people through it all. There, you can witness growth, brotherhoods formed around men of different races growing vegetables together and spiritual development for women culminating in a weekend retreat on a beautiful Indiana lake. Twenty years of service and they have only begun to serve. What an honor it has been for me to be a part of the programs from the beginning. I remember in the beginning the Cafe's roof seemed to spring a new leak with each rain storm. The Cafe went on never missing a beat because when it rained, they knew where to place the big buckets. Elease was confident that all repairs were in excellent hands … "No worry here" is how she handled it.

I remember when several non-profits years ago wanted to conduct 30 hours of survival life skills training for mothers coming out of prison, being reunited with their children, and living in our neighborhood. These ten women and their children were blessed because they deserved it, and this cafe figured it out a long time ago, that when all the resources work together for the good of those with needs, then miracles happen. Well, we asked Elease if we could hold these evening classes at the cafe. Some of the women had jobs during the day and they were overjoyed to start providing for their children, whom they had missed during years of incarceration. One of the non-profits involved provided new clothes and coats for the whole family. Without any hesitation, Elease said, "It will be wonderful, mothers and their children here at the cafe working together over the next five weeks to get them ready to make that transition."

I will never forget how special the Cafe made their graduation and the bond the women developed with each other and their children. Some of the women had completed their time and after the graduation they caught buses to Chicago and other places.

Every neighborhood deserves a place like the Cafe where you can become empowered and embrace healing, no matter where you are on your personal journey. This is a place that welcomes you and your healing. The Unleavened Bread Cafe is there to help you do the hard work it sometimes takes to overcome. This is a place where you can give back in life working alongside volunteers who came through the programs. These volunteers can speak truth to power. I meet people at the cafe all the time who feel they are just a vessel. They thank any participants looking for the right bus to board for their opportunity to serve.

LYNDA SKIPPER

Lynda is a community activist who has taught survival skills classes for women at the Unleavened Bread Cafe. Lynda is also a grant writer who has written grants for surrounding churches. She is a proud mother of one daughter.

KIM WALKER

The Pain I Still Maintain

Anger is the pain I still maintain.
Anger has caused me a lot of physical, emotional,
mental and spiritual pain.

I wonder what it would have been like.
If my mother would have allowed God to deal with
the anger in her heart.

Would it have made a difference in my life?
Now that I am an adult?

I have held onto a lot of things I saw my mother do
like verbal abuse that has no use.
I thought it would help me ease the pain
I still maintain.

So as I tell this story, how I almost allowed the devil
to take away God's glory.

I moved into a house unmarried. I thought
it would be my home,
but all we did was fuss, bicker and throw stones.
Stones with words that hurt and harmed each other
and pierced both our souls.
—I did this with my daughter as well—
Now the damage is done, neither one of us including
my daughter has won.

Now nothing's going right. That spirit of anger
that brings about the verbal abuse
won't let me sleep at night.

The anger left unchecked has a deep bitter root in my soul.
The words I spoke
has caused these two relationships to fold. The damage
I done by using cuss words.
Damn, the devil has won.

This ain't no fun,
allowing the devil to take over my mind
and say things to the people I love that was so unkind.

I forgot that God said the battle is already won.
That I don't have to use the verbal abuse that has no use to
maintain the pain because of the hurt and harm
that was caused as a child that my Momma allowed.

My mother been forgiven and I have too.
I heard that still small voice say,
It's time to let go, my child, of the verbal abuse.
Can't you see by now it has no use
and has caused you a lot of inner pain.

It's time to edify the ones you love,
don't carry that generational curse no longer.

Allow my spirit that lives inside of you to become stronger.

So I got down on my knees, folded my hands, repented
and started to pray.

Holy Spirit, make me stronger,
take away the anger in my heart that I still maintain
so I don't have to use the verbal abuse that has no use.

I threw up my hands, told the Lord I'm finally willing
to surrender.

I can see the pain and strife in my life from the verbal abuse.
Yes Lord, I agree it has no use.
I'm so so sorry, forgive me.

On that day He took my pain away,
that I still maintain from the verbal abuse.
Now my life is changed.

KIM WALKER

These words I share are from a song by Yolanda Adams. "Before I tell them, Lord please tell me. Before I tell it my way, sit me down, make me silent and give it to me your way. Before I reach out to them, Lord reach out to me."

The inner voice that allows me to put pen to the paper is the Spirit of God that lives inside of me, He does not just want to heal me from the hardship and heart aches of life. He wants to heal others as well so he has afforded me another opportunity to write a poem from my pain not my intellect.

I would like to acknowledge once again Marian University Writing Professor Wendy and every intern that participated in the second year of *Voices Unlocked Soulful Stories from 30th and Central.*

TIA WASHUM

The Children

God never shows or reveals the parents or the people that will guide, mold or love us through this journey of life. What happened to the laughter of the children? The TV shows Sammy Terri and Captain Kangaroo. The game Mother May I, Duck, Duck, Goose, Red light, Green light—Stop!

What happened when I stopped being a child? Is it when someone told me I was beautiful? I laughed until that individual touched me in disturbing ways that affected my mind, my body, and most of all my innocence. The laughter stopped. I asked, "Why did you touch me like that!?" Because I remember when the laughter stopped for me. I once was a child, I too watched those TV shows, I also played those games that children played. I laughed all the time.

Remember when you hit your first home run or your first three point shot that made you the hero of the basketball team? What happened? When you won the spelling bee contest, and let's not forget about the science fair. What happened?! Was it when you touched me, you felt you could get your innocence back? Did it make you feel eighty feet tall? Did you relive that moment when you were the hero of the team?

Remember, Remember, Remember! The children, their laughter, the smiles. What is wrong could be made right! God doesn't always reveal life on life's terms, or situations to our understanding, but he does forgive, guide, love, and mold us through this journey called life. That's what happens. Remember.

TIA WASHUM

Tia R. Washum (Womack), aka Diana, was born in Indianapolis, Indiana on December 28, 1963, she is the eldest of three children: one brother and two sisters. She has four children, two boys and two girls, from the ages of 21 to 33. She also has two beautiful grandsons, ages three and six. Tia works with sexually abused and chemically dependent children to help them find a new way to live with their past experiences. She loves working out, playing basketball, zip lining, and bike riding, etc. She loves cooking, traveling, and writing.

Rain Water

The Spirit of God was moving over the face of the waters.

~ Genesis 1:2

When I think about the rain water, my mother comes to mind. She would wash the hair of my sisters and me with the rain water. Then she would use cut up pieces of brown paper bags to roll our hair with. This is how she would get us ready for Sunday School the next morning, but only when it rained. Otherwise, she would just wash it with faucet water.

When I am sleeping, I hear the sound of the water and it makes me relax. When I get a massage, I hear the sound of the ocean. Rain water can be cleansing. I love to stand in the rain and smell it. Rain helps things to grow, like trees and flowers. But it can destroy or bring life. When I think about the Bible, during the time of Noah's Ark, it rained for forty days and forty nights.

Rain water makes me feel like I am in a safe place. It can make you want to be in a quiet place, to write, to read, and to pray in a quiet place. That way you can hear from God and get answers. We have had many beautiful gardens from the rain water.

ELEASE WOMACK

    I am widow with three children, two girls and one son, eight grandchildren and five great-grandchildren. I love hospitality, cooking, helping others. For the last twenty years, I have nourished the community at the Unleavened Bread Cafe. I am very grateful to work with the women—they are my passion in life.

The Women's Writing Workshop in Action

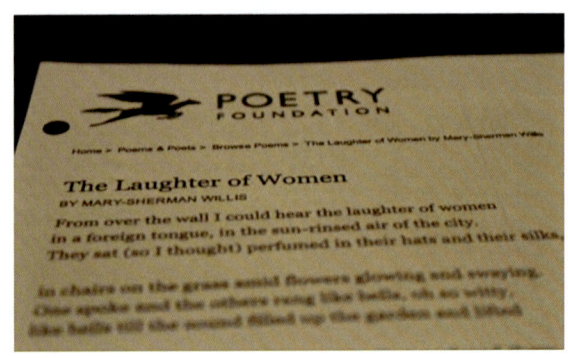

From *Voices Unlocked: Soulful Stories from 30th & Central*

TIA WASHUM

The Day the Laughter Stopped

I remember the day the laughter stopped. It was a snowy, cold, and dreary day. All I could see was the cold gray white scenery as the snow was slowly blowing. The streetlight was changing: green, yellow, and red, green, yellow, and red. All I could think about was the day the laughter stopped. Where did it go? We were just in Big Ree's basement. Big Ree, a.k.a., Aretha Franklin.

* * *

The first day of Spring Break, me and my girls: Shelley, Barbara, and me—Big Ree, Natalie Cole, and me, Diana Ross, in the basement. I can see Big Ree with the hairbrush microphone. Her right hand shimmering to the box-shaped record player that only plays the 45s and LPs. As Ree was singing, Natalie and me lip-synched behind her, *Chain, chain, chain, chain of fools*....I remember Shell crying, I don't know if it was because of the laughter or the alcohol. The washer was cycling in the background, the air smelled with the fresh scent of Downy.

Feeling the music, I see my friend lifting up her hand, shimmering as she's feeling the music. We're all feeling the music. The light fixture is swinging, a long cord and a light bulb with no shade over it as we are doing the be-bop to *What you baby I got it, what you need, baby I got it.* Shelly is in the front just bursting out, and Barbara and me are uncontrollably laughing as we're backup singers doing the hitchhiker. Our thumbs flying, our feet moving. I would love for her to call my name, *"Teeee!"* That's what she called me with a big smile. I would return and say, *"Sheeeellll."*

* * *

I remember the day. It was cold and dreary. The street was quiet, the first day of heavy snow. The streetlights were changing: green, yellow, and red. It took me a long time to pay my respects to the family. All I could see was the cold gray and white scenery. All I could think of was my friend, my Homie, was gone as the center of the 45 cracked. No more of Big Ree, Natalie, and me.

Fair Warning

In a desolate community, on a road with no name
In a place where no one even accidentally came
Lies a small little house in the middle of nowhere
Where I hid my box and only I know it's there

My box is quite small for as much as it holds
And is so worn from use, it has tape on the folds
Although the box top was tattered it still served its use
Cause the feelings it creates cannot be reproduced

My box holds my secrets, my box holds my pain
My box holds my disgrace, my dishonor, my shame
My box holds the obstacles that stand in my way
My box holds the things I can't deal with today

So if you're in the middle of nowhere, hopelessly lost
In a desolate community please leave at all cost
Don't ask for directions until there are names on the road
And please, don't go looking for where my box is stowed.

JENNIFER FENTRESS

Jennifer Fentress is a young, creative poet who introduces a strong sense of sound, rhythm, rhyme and wordplay into her poems. Jennifer discovered that writing was a helpful way to deal with the emotional pain of being a survivor of domestic violence. She is a recent graduate from IUPUI and is hopeful about the future. Jennifer enjoys home cooked meals, car rides, and Mountain Dew.

I am eternally grateful for the writing workshop because it gives me a place to express myself without fear of rejection. It is located in the neighborhood and allows a group of women to meet, socialize and bounce ideas off each other. The writing workshop ultimately became a safe place to inspire like-minded people to open their minds enough to create the beautiful pieces of poetry and prose showcased in this book.

ELEASE WOMACK

Wearing My Mother's Mantle

I am from Indianapolis, born in a house at 1902 Miller Street. My parents are Samuel and Johnnie B. Williams. We have a Southern background. I am from a family of good cooks on both sides. My father's side was all educators, business people, and hard workers.

* * *

I learned what love was from my mother and father; discipline, correcting me, clothing, and feeding me. The correction I got was not putting a belt, or their hands on me, although the Bible said "Spare the rod or spoil the child." My parents put good family values in me.

* * *

I learned to cook when I was a teenager. Watching my mother and father, I would ask a question about measuring cups. But they didn't use measuring cups. They were natural cooks and used coffee cups and regular teaspoons. When I got to high school, I took Foods and learned to measure my food. I have been cooking ever since.

* * *

My mother, Johnnie B., was a woman of God. She had many gifts. Not only did she help older people in the home like cooking or cleaning, she would help children with activities in the evening. Today we would call it extended care or after school programs. She started a group in Indianapolis and called it Northside Community Missionary Society. My mother and her group would raise money so at Christmas time they would go to the Welfare Department and pick a family they could help. They would take them to J. C. Penney's on Monument Circle to buy them clothes, and then they would take them to Frisch's Big Boy on Market and Illinois Streets for lunch. They did great work in communities.

The work I am doing today my mother did back in the late 40's and early 50's. It is still giving; I am wearing her mantle.

My father, Samuel Williams, came to Indianapolis in 1922. He met my mother here. He didn't talk about love a lot; they were modest and I never saw them kiss. But I still knew.

Samuel was a man of integrity, honest and very stern. He rented a room when he first got here. He found a job working on the railroad out by Kentucky Ave, at Smith Chemical. He worked there 40 years. He helped build Plant Five at Allison's, and after it was finished they offered him a job. He declined because he loved working outdoors.

* * *

My grandmother on my mother's side, Lulabell, was about 75 years of age when she died. She was a grand person who had 10 children, all born at home with a midwife in Cordele, Georgia. She would use Red Seal snuff after breakfast using the can as a spittoon. My grandmother didn't work; she was a stay-at-home mother, teaching her children and grandchildren to work, clean house, and wash clothing. That was also where they learned to cook. She made their clothes. My mother and grandmother would wear housedresses with bib aprons and cotton stockings. They kept handkerchiefs or towels to wipe away the sweat of summer. Johnnie B. and her father came to Indianapolis when she was 16 to save money to go back to Georgia to get her mother and the other children. My grandmother's children took care of her when she got older because my grandfather had passed. They couldn't find birth certificates, and so she could not get Social Security. My grandmother was a woman of wisdom.

* * *

Over 35 years ago I received Christ in my life. The minister said, "Who were you when Jesus was crucified? Were you Pontius Pilate? Were you Peter who denied him three times? Or were you one of the Jews who crucified him?" All I could say was, "I have joy, unspeakable joy in my heart." I was so happy I couldn't keep it to myself.

I love to show love by giving, because love is action. I love hospitality.

Market Street

Market Street: 1955, St. Louis.
Store fronts, tenement buildings
filled with, caresses, indifference,
worn from age, profuse with
the presence of home.

To me the tenements transposed into palaces
overrun with lords and ladies of the era; they were cast
to parade and stroll through my 8-year-old mind.
Like winds of change, they excited and tickled me!

Mamie, the apple of my eye, spoke to me through her doings:
always hugged me until I couldn't breathe,
warmed the quilt for the bed at night.
Each room burst with aromas of time and place.

The large kitchen eternally integrated with whiffs of
collard greens, baked ham, cornbread, chicken, pig skins,
chitlins, pot roast, and homemade chicken soup,
all to consume my heart with nourishment.
Under Mamie's large kitchen table lived a big ol' dog
named PP whom we fed from scraps of tenderness
that Mamie primed especially for her
without help from Purina.

Late afternoon sunlight sprayed the living room,
awarding the sofa, chairs, tables, and figurines

with illumination through the shutterless windows.
Views on Market Street through those windows captured a
snapshot of the numbers man
coming down the street with Mamie's hit.
The broadcast news had already alerted us
that Mamie won on a nickel.
Yea, this meant tonight was party night!
The living room was filled with the ladies and lords
of Market Street.
Being all ears I could hear everything.
Doc., Janie, Brother, and BeBe biding, trump, jack, nine spot.
In the middle of the floor Ronnie and Darcy,
created some 'shake, rattle, and roll'
to St. Louisianan Chuck Berry singing
"Maybelline Why Can't You Be True."
Sarah and Carl were drunk on too much whiskey
in the corner and gossiping about the new family
down on Market Street.
They said the joint was jumping.

Before the guests left the party, it was mandatory
that leftover stamina be used to clean the living room
to eliminate the smells of colognes, sweat,
cigarettes, and leftover food.
Once the living room was refreshed
with the perfume of Balm in Gilead, it was bed time.

Mamie's bedroom always smelled of warm subdued feelings,
snug powders, and old quilts heated in front
of the kitchen oven.
The quilts always served as my boat, tent, tepee, house,
or whatever fantasy I had created
to lull me to sleep and then the next day

play it out down by Union Station on Market Street.
My fantasies were always musicals, dramas. I, the thespian,
the director, writer, producer and the audience,always
captured the people I would see
at the *Meeting of Waters*
across from Union Station, St. Louis 1955.
After a night bountiful with characters,
I attired myself with clothes that would be easy to embellish
for my character as I ran to the *Meeting of Waters*
across from Union Station, St. Louis, 1955.
At twilight, I decided to jump in the water
with the fish and spirits.
I played in what I now know to be
Man and Woman,
sculptures representing the Mississippi and the Missouri.
The mermaids and the fish were standing as the tributaries,
flowing into and through the river.

I wanted to prepare myself for the journey home.
I am still in character,
a mermaid running around the pool along the edge.

Once everyone was gone, I stood in the water.
I splashed around and touched the sculptures.
As the streetlights slowly and softly came on,
that was a signal for a change in character,
a notice to drop the bottle-caps I had used as scales.

No longer could I be a mermaid
across from Union Station, Market Street, 1955.

JENDAYI MAYIBUYE

    Jendayi Mayibuye - 68 years young, mother of three sons, 14 grandchildren, and four great grandchildren and a personal relationship with Christ. Social worker by trade and licensed addictions counselor.

    The writing class was a valuable tool that unleashed my inner voice and taught me the discipline of creativity. Applause to Marian University and Professor Wendy, along with her photographer, artist, and writing interns, Lydia, K.C., Hannah, Moriah, and Lori. I also want to thank Mother Elease Womack for her tireless dedication to the women and people of her community.

KIM WALKER

Crack, Cracked, & God Took Me Back

Why did you call me all those names?
I was a child and felt so ashamed.
Ashamed of my life and who I was supposed to be
Especially since I did not know my Daddy,
Not knowing I had a heavenly father watching over me.
You did not know the self-harm was going to start,
The crack, the prostitution that dominated my heart.
You thought, and I thought, my life was over,
But little did we both know that was the beginning of my story.

My story,
The pain that I went through.
You see,
For a long time I treated myself to death.
I remember the seizures
The jerking of my arm.
I tried to control it,
But I couldn't.
My eyes begin to roll in the back of my head

I'm losing consciousness

I am tired of using crack,
The prostitution.

I was born in his image,
Precious in his sight.

These are the words I should have held onto.
As I try to rest my mind so I don't have to think about
how I allowed all those men to do things with my body
that were so inhuman.

I'm crying and screaming from being dragged across the concrete.
Then his fist hit my face,
POW!!!
I fell to the ground.

Death you thought you had me.

I'm not talking about physical death,
It's spiritual (I survived)

Death did not know I was chosen before the beginning of time.
That God said in his word,
"Kim's not supposed to die."

Weak, drained, almost insane.
I love you O'Lord,
My strength,

Crack, cracked, but God took me back.

I survived.

The Lives in These Bones:
Tributes to Elease and the Unleavened
Bread Cafe

Being Elease's biological daughter, I'm blessed. The way I look at it, God loved me so much he gave a mother to me, like her, to help me in my walk of life. But I didn't know she would be that walk of life for other people, and they would call her mother. But it's exciting. It's a wonderful experience to have a mother like her who not only imparts in me but into all people, all women. I'm glad. It's hard following in her shoes though, let me say that. But I'm glad the example I have is my mother, that's my hero.

The good works she does—I know they are in me too and I try to do the same thing. It's not easy sharing the kind of mother that I have. But what I've found out is everybody is searching for some type of love, and she has that type of love, to not just give to me but to everybody.

The cafe is a place of restoration. It is a place where people come together. You know, if you want a taste of the Kingdom—it doesn't matter what color you are, we are all diverse here—come to the Unleavened Bread Cafe. The cafe is like a reservoir, and the Bible says that because it's a place to get replenished. It's just a place where everyone can come together to help one another. A place of peace. If you have things really pulling you down, you are going to leave here with a smile. I think that's why I really come.

~ Tia

I'm excited to be 80 and have been able to be a part of the cafe. I was glad to get a cup of coffee for Einar—this man never quit. Elease has a conscientious attitude and is firm about God's business and His love for people, which came from our mom. Elease will help you to the end. She is going to give you the whole nine yards' version of hope. I love Thanksgiving and Christmas. It is especially moving when she gives out to the neighborhood during the holidays.

When I go down to the cafe and want her to myself, it is so hard (and I get jealous sometimes) because she is so busy. I know better now that this is her calling, it is God's business and it is what he appointed her to do. Elease gives people confidence and hope, I admire that about her.

~ Claudine Jones

I am the woman of God that I am today thanks to the word of God, the Bethlehem House, and thanks to the Unleavened Bread Café and its proprietor, Mother Elease Womack. Having worked for her, with her, and under her these past ten years, I saw her apply daily what the scriptures say about loving people and how to treat people. She exemplified the word of God and the application of God's word in day to day life. All the glory, honor, and praise to God for his placement of her in my life. I could not have made it this far without Him and without her.

~ A Miracle Named Jackie

Do you know? Have you not heard? How many lives you have touched with your life and sharing God's word?

Where do I get my girl power, where do I get my strength? From Mother Elease Womack.

Even though you may have not seen her struggles, hurt and pain but she was still able to maintain 20 years of hope for our tomorrow, showing us women that we can make it no matter what the sorrow. So that's where I get my girl power, and that's where I get my strength. Right here at The Unleavened Bread Cafe. Thank you, Mother, for having my voice unlocked, soulful stories on 30th and Central Street.

~ Kim Walker

I was a scrawny little girl broken in many places, seeking recovery from the disease I had within myself. I chased Jackie (woo-woo) and Rita Rita. In the chasing, I often came to the Unleavened Bread Cafe where I soon found God setting me up for living. Mama was sitting at the round table as she often does. I came in and explained I needed to do community service. She said, "Sure baby, let me get a hug."

I felt a sense of relief when I let go. There were two other gentlemen at the table and she said, "We are about to go pray, would you like to join us?" I said sure, being raised up in church, prayer was always important. I sat down, bowed my head, and closed my eyes. As mother prayed I could feel tears streaming down my face. Could it be God talkin' to me? I then felt a fire in my hands like someone had lit a match. I cried even harder. Here my spiritual mama was praying for a broken-hearted child, not knowing that at the end of the prayer I would dedicate my life to Christ and be baptized two hours later. I went in unclean, and came out a new creature in Christ.

Over the years, I have watched my spiritual mama love the unlovable, feed the children, young and old, pray for and heal the brokenhearted, and speak life into the hopeless. When I see her, I see a God-fearing, faith-filled women who is selfless, loving, kind-hearted, peaceful, and definitely long-suffering. She blesses the ones that have lost hope (I was one). She gives us a safe place, for both men and women. Most of all she always has a smile and a big Jesus hug for everyone who comes to the Cafe. I am honored and blessed to have a mentor who constantly shows the love of Jesus. She doesn't talk it, she walks it and lives it. Isaiah 61:1-4 reminds me of her.

My spiritual mama's natural and spiritual children sit under her and glean and learn how to be a model for Christ! That's my spiritual mama.

~ Vickie Armour

I would go to Tabernacle Church, down the street. When I would drive down Central, there were two phones on each corner, there were eight phones. Those phones were really busy, because those were the main deal phones. People get on the phone, then wait five minutes, then somebody come and have some transactions. So I started stopping up the street a little bit, seeing what was going on, and at some point I thought, We need to do something here. This building was for sale. Southern Star Baptist Church had moved closer to the downtown, to a new building, and were selling this one. Something told me, well, maybe we could put a cafe here, or something. And I noticed that a lot of the guys in the neighborhood here, would be walking up and down the sidewalk. I thought to myself, maybe we can create some jobs down here. And then it just kind of evolved.

I think it was John Mills who came up with the name Interwoven by Jesus, we were woven by Jesus, so we called the not-for-profit Interwoven by Jesus. And Elease came up with the name Unleavened Bread.

We decided to open the door, that we should have coffee and donuts. And the guys started coming. Right off the bat, we had a bunch of guys, guys walking up and down sidewalk, and they'd come and work on the floor, work on this, you know, no pay, they just wanted to be a part of it.

There was a concrete wall there, and John just kind of, he's a special character, and he said, there's going to be a door there. Within a few hours, he had an opening, a door in between.

At one point, Tom said, "I wouldn't buy the matches to burn this place down. That's what he said first. He didn't like anything that he saw. But then he came in 100 percent."

~ Einar Stefansson

It's been a real blessing to us, to the neighborhood and to lots of people, and to me too. Miss Elease, she's a joy.

~ Lena Stefansson

I gave it three months. We've been down this road before, I kept saying to myself, trying to organize things in the community. I've said this many times, "I'll give it three months. And my goodness, here it is 20 years."

I was a social worker, I was taught to, "You got a problem, Elease, you need to make an appointment and come and see me, and I'll fix it." Baloney. It doesn't work that way. That's really not what social work is. It took the Unleavened Bread Cafe and that experience, in my case, and I'm not the only one, in my case as a trained social worker, to realize that that's what social services really were all about. I'm happy with what I learned at IU, but I've forgotten most of it. If I ever was effective, what made me so was experiences like I had on the street with people on the street and especially at the Cafe.

Elease, I love you for everything you've done. Thank you. You've really changed my life. I assume this, I don't know, but I was on my way up, I was Head of the Social Work department at IU, my goodness, everybody was looking up to Dr. Metzger and Dr. Metzger that. Elease and the Cafe taught me more than any other entity in my life, to listen. To hear things I wasn't really hearing before. I could have been Dean of the School of Social Work the rest of my life, but that wouldn't have meant a thing. My work with the Cafe is clearly the most meaningful experience I've had. I hesitate to call it work, yes, it's work, but my, it turned out to be so wonderful.

~ David Metzger

To my sister and friend in Christ:

I just want to take time out to congratulate you on your twenty years of ministry. I can remember when God birthed the ministry to you. You have been a blessing to your community, you have fed and clothed those in need, given them a place to get clean and to lay their heads. You are a blessing to the Kingdom. It was all for the Glory of God. I know that He is shining on you and you have Crowns in Heaven.

~ Dorothy Flowers

The Unleavened Bread Cafe is a healing place for lost souls in need of restoration. When I lived in Indianapolis, I used to volunteer as a cook, cashier, and dishwasher. Being in the atmosphere was life changing. It is more than a place that serves good food; your soul is truly fed. The Mother and founder, Elease Womack, who happens to be my Godmother, is the matriarch of that neighborhood and everybody knows her. I am honored to have been a part of history in the hood where you can love, live, and lead like Christ.

~ Alesha Puckett

It was a rainy day in 2001 and Duwaafie said, "Let's stop in to get something to eat." She said they had great fish and soup, and they were having prayer on the other side. I was thinking, "What kind of restaurant is this?" Then someone said, "It's not just a restaurant, it's a ministry."

In October of 2015, we moved a block down and since then, I come to the Cafe often, so I know it to truly be a ministry and a blessing.

~ Darjshai Jordan

The Place

The Unleavened Bread Cafe, The Place where the outside screams of brightness and beauty, then welcomes you in. The Place where friends and community are Cafe family, gathered to pray and break bread together, and give comfort to those in need. It is The Place of blessed harmony and peace. It is The Place where voices rise with laughter of love and joy. For some, it is The Place where you can learn, thrive, and start a new life. You hear songs of praise coming from its community room, preparing you for a great celebration of gratitude. Speakers come to spread the good neighbor news to the Circle of Friends, every first Tuesday. Good food is prepared by those kitchen angels, pleasing the palate and keeping you coming back. And over it all is the 'boss angel', our Elease, with her powerful will; making magic, using her gracious hospitality, good humor, friendly and enlightened conversation in The Place.

~ Carol L. Evans

Ms. Elease you are an inspiration to all of us who seek to be present to others in a spiritual way. Your heart wrote the book about how to welcome others and love in ways that matter. Thank you for what you have done in our community and in particular with the students at Marian, and for me!

~ Jeanne Hildago

Elease is a wonderful grandmother to all people. She is always willing to reach out to people in need. She is street-wise in terms of welcoming them and enabling them to come together as a group; both the staff and people who come in. She really does love every individual.

~ Dick Hamilton

I have lived in Mapleton-Fall Creek since 1981, so I have seen many changes through my various roles as a resident, a member of the Neighborhood Association Board, Editor of the old MFC Gazette, and various roles at the Mapleton-Fall Creek Community Development Cooperation. I can recall the derelict buildings that were at the corner for a long time, once the old drug store and the car repair dealership went out of business. I have helped to raise funds for the Cafe, and to sing its praises! When I was on the city council, it was a place to hear from folks about what they needed from their city.

The Cafe is a product of the local community, not a chain that tried to come in and failed because it lacked the spirit it takes to grow roots in a community. There are few places of public interaction in Mapleton, places where one can meet a friend, make a friend, and share bread with a friend; these are critical things for a community, and the Cafe has been one of the only places for these experiences. The Cafe is rooted in its belief in people and their innate goodness, and it has offered, through Elease's vision, chances for folks who need another chance, and that has been a starting over point for many.

~ Jackie Nytes

Our organization, Faith and Labor Coalition, has been meeting here for 12-15 years. The organization formed over 15 years ago to work on social and economic justice issues for working families. We chose this venue because it's in a neighborhood that is so economically challenged and because of the Cafe's mission. "It is home for us."

Elease is an angel. She's one of God's angels walking among us. She doesn't just talk the talk, she goes over and above. Everyone calls her Mother Elease because she makes us all so comfortable and welcome.

~ Nancy Holly

The Cafe is an island of community-building and connecting people to each other. It's a hope. The Cafe brought blacks and whites, young and old, varying levels of education together, a remarkable mix of what community can be. We live in a culture built on the concept of money, but the Cafe is built on the love for people, it's not here to make money, but it needs to stay open—like a breath of fresh air for the society and a love of community. Elease is the anchor of the Cafe. Without her, this place would not survive. She is the "Hugger-in-Chief." Elease's hug embraces everybody and is a symbol of the Cafe, which embraces everybody

Someone in a tree nursery business planted an evergreen tree, digging through soil and rocks. The tree was planted here (the tree had so many hard times, sometimes people drive off the sidewalk and knock or bent over). The perseverance of the tree became a symbol of the Cafe; despite being knocked around, it remains there.

~ John Gibson

Elease and the Cafe has provided food for people who don't have money, provided food for Thanksgiving and Christmas, arranged to provide food for prisoners and their families when they go to visit from the community via the prison bus, and provided space for classes and meeting space for many types of meetings (like our spiritual studies book club). The Cafe also provided jobs for people who have had trouble finding work. I believe in the Cafe because of all the wonderful things I have seen happen there.

Elease is a wonderful, big-hearted provider of hugs for ALL people. She had a vision that has come to fruition and impacted the lives of many, many people.

~ Barb Griffen

The Cafe provides a steadfast presence of welcome and care in a struggling community. It brings the resources from the community itself into the light. There is the outreach to women, families, seniors, the wandering, and the homeless. It provides space for lives to change and ideas to grow. The writing group is a wonderful example of this! The overarching theme is realizing God's love for His people through His Word, His hand, and His bounty. It is creative, responsive, and energizing.

Elease walks in praise. She has a heart for the poor, the broken, and the disenfranchised. She is affectionate, likes to laugh, cook, and give hugs. She is a friend to many, and a mother to more than even she knows.

~ Esther Horvath-Fer

The Unleavened Bread Cafe found me in the fall of 2004. Upon entering the building at 30th and Central, I felt I was now on holy ground. What I needed, I would find right here. Over the past thirteen years, I have received so many spiritual gifts here at the Cafe. I was blessed to serve as a board president, and I am currently a board member.

~ David Volker

Where can I start—there have been so many good, positive vibes that have made me a better person. Mother Elease's passion is so deep, it rubs off on you. She is the epitome of a true, strong woman. Her heart never stops beating love. She makes you feel so good. She stayed faithful to the Cafe, and I just remember the love that you feel when you walk into the Unleavened Bread Cafe. I have grown stronger in my faith because of Mother Elease Womack.

~ Leslie Allen

We see the Unleavened Bread Cafe as an extension of our ministry. We would claim the Cafe as our own, just as the Cafe would claim Tab as its own. It is my hope that the community will continue to diversify without leaving anyone behind, always welcoming anyone in, for the diversity of our community makes us richer rather than poorer.

My fondest memories of the Cafe have to do with faith and fellowship, the feeding of the body and the feeding of the soul. We all need a mother who will warmly embrace us no matter where we've been or what we have done, lead us home, and direct us to a path of restoration. Elease has been that, and still is, for countless people. In many ways, Elease is our spiritual mother. We will always be grateful for her heart for the Lord. Elease is His hands and feet.

~ Rev. L. John Gable

I got involved with the Cafe in 2002. We were launching the Bethlehem House community groups, and the Cafe afforded us a perfect conduit into the community. The Cafe provides food for the soul as well for the body, and thus a ministry. The Cafe serves the most vulnerable amongst us. Elease is a warm, loving community spiritual mother.

~ Nate Rush

Of course, some members of the Mid-North Shepherd's Center had heard about the wonderful ministry of the Unleavened Bread Cafe. They had heard that the Cafe freely offers hugs and love along with cups of hot coffee for those coming from a night; perhaps on the streets, or trying to sleep in a cold house without money to pay the gas bill or a variety of other reasons. We heard that no one was turned away.

~ Dorothy Gerner

Our collaboration started when a good friend of mine, brother Bobby Weddington, had shared with me he wanted me to meet a person in the neighborhood and this was Mother Elease. Our ministry was birthed under the wings of the Unleavened Bread that highlighted first, our daily Bible study, prayer meetings, and later on, our church fellowship to the Mapleton-Fall Creek Community. Now that our ministry has grown and flourished, we still make our way back to where it all started. I am thankful for the humble beginning of seeing, sharing, and sowing because of what I have received from Mother (Elease) and this atmosphere. To God be the Glory.

~ Pastor Joseph L. Reaves Jr.

Twenty years ago, I was with a group holding a tent revival at the lot catty-corner to the Cafe. Elease had opened the restroom to us, and that's when I met her. She approached me about teaming up to have classes for women making a fresh start; how to leave the past behind, heal the wounds of the heart, and embrace the future God has tailor-made for them. That's how Freedoms Fire was born, eight years ago.

It is incredible how every individual, whether they be a city councilman or a homeless lady on the street, are greeted by Elease with the same embrace, full of Christ's love and respect. People of all denominations leave their differences at the door, meet together, and work in one accord towards bettering the community and meeting its needs.

~ Holly Webb

The Unleavened Bread Cafe has been a meeting place for all kinds of community activism groups, a catalyst for people sharing and organizing ideas for the entire time it's been here. This is my church. It's been an anchor in my life for the last twenty years of renewal, hope, and friendship.

~ Bob Proctor

Selections from the Unleavened Bread Cafe's Scrapbook

INDIANAPOLIS
BUSINESS JOURNAL

APRIL 7-13, 1997   VOL. 18 NO. 1 • 44 PAGES   © IBJ CORP 1997 • LOCALLY OWNED $1.25

Elease Womack is cooking up more than breakfast at The Unleavened Bread Cafe.

IBJ PHOTO/ROBIN JERSTAD

Nourishing a neighborhood

Cafe brings life to 30th and Central

BY STEPHEN BEAVEN
IBJ REPORTER

Elease Womack's new restaurant isn't in what retail real estate brokers would call a prime spot.

The area around 30th Street and Central Avenue is dominated by boarded-up storefronts, empty lots and billboards advertising liquor. A few weeks ago, there was a shooting nearby.

But, Womack says, it is the perfect place for The Unleavened Bread Cafe. She and her partners in the not-for-profit restaurant want to nourish the neighborhood. Their cafe will provide affordable—sometimes free—food, office space for a couple of small businesses, job opportunities, a place to pray, and a respite from the street.

Womack talks of reaching out to drug addicts, alcoholics and prostitutes "just to let them know there's hope," she says.

"All of them won't come to church. But some of them will

▶ See BREAD page 18A

THE
Unleavened Bread
CAFE

DINE IN or CARRY OUT at THIS PLACE
3001 N. Central • 317-920-5292

The Unleavened Bread Cafe
BIBLE SCHOOL

The Unleavened Bread Cafe
SUPPER of HOPE

The Unleavened Bread Cafe
TEEN HARVESTERS

'Mother Womack' is feeding souls at this Indy cafe

Matthew Tully
Columnist

As he walked out of the Unleavened Bread Cafe on Wednesday afternoon, a customer named Rick Reel told me what to expect.

"You get a hug with every meal," he said.

Inside, about a dozen people sat at the nonprofit cafe's tables. Men and women. Young and old. Black and white. But from the moment I walked in, it was clear who was in charge. That would be the 71-year-old woman sitting at a round table near the front counter, talking to a recovering drug addict, offering him words of hope.

The woman's name is Elease Womack. But, she said, "Everybody calls me Mother Womack."

Mother Womack had spotted a stranger in the room — that would be me — and offered a smile and then a seat next to her. I took it, curious to hear the story of this curious cafe that's tucked within the Mapleton Fall Creek neighborhood.

It's a neighborhood that has plen-

» See TULLY, Page 6A

MATTHEW TULLY/THE STAR
Elease Womack founded the Unleavened

The Newby Oval cycle track, a quarter-mile white-pine board velodrome, was built for $23,000 in 1898 by Arthur Newby. THE NEWS 1926 FILE PHOTO

Awards & Recognitions

Distinguished Service Award, Fidelity Lodge Fifty-five, F. & A.A.-P.H.A.

Jurisdiction of Indiana, November 12, 2016

Communities Building Community with Judy O'Bannon, October 16, 2016

Valuable Contribution to the Community, October 16, 2016

Certificate of Appreciation from Taste of Courage, October 10, 2016

Lucious Newsome Community Legacy Award, January 11, 2013

Clothe-a-Child Committee, December 2, 2012

The Council City of Indianapolis, Marion County, January 24, 2011

Mayor's Community Service Award, November 4, 2009

The Spirit of the Lord God is upon me; because the Lord hath anointed me to preach good tidings unto the meek; he hath sent me to bind up the brokenhearted, to proclaim liberty to the captives, and the opening of the prison to them that are bound; To proclaim the acceptable year of the Lord, and the day of vengeance of our God; to comfort all that mourn; To appoint unto them that mourn in Zion, to give unto them beauty for ashes, the oil of joy for mourning, the garment of praise for the spirit of heaviness; that they might be called trees of righteousness, the planting of the Lord, that he might be glorified. And they shall build the old wastes, they shall raise up the former desolations, and they shall repair the waste cities, the desolations of many generations.

~ Isaiah 61: 1-4